# THE CACTUS BOOK

LEAH TROLLER

I see the fruit.

I see the seeds.

I see the bird.

I see the dirt.

I see the cactus.

I see the roots.

I see the rain.

I see the needles.

I see the flowers.

# LIFE OF A CACTUS

7

Cacti produce tasty fruit and flowers to attract animals like bats. Bats help to produce cactus seeds by pollinating cactus flowers.

1

Seeds

2
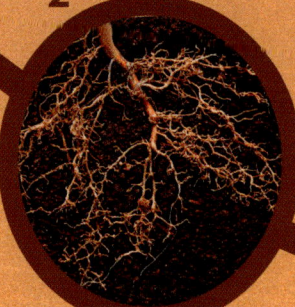
Roots

3

Baby Cactus

6 Fruit
5 Flowers
4 Adult Cactus

13

# CACTUS FACTS

There are about 2,000 different species of cactus.

The roots of a cactus grow more outward than downward. This helps them take in as much rainwater as possible.

An adult saguaro cactus can grow as tall as 45 feet!

The needles of a cactus are better at storing and keeping water than leaves.

Cactus fruit is a popular food. You may find it in your grocery store!

# POWER WORDS

**How many can you read?**

I

see

the

# MATCHING

I can use the first letter sound to match the word to the picture.

dirt
seeds
cactus
bird
flowers